C O N T E N T S

GH00986244

2

A silent man in lifes affairs
A thinker from a Boy
A Peasant in his daily cares—
The Poet in his joy

from 'The Peasant Poet'

John Clare, Northamptonshire's 'peasant poet', was a self-educated genius. He was acutely sensitive to the rhythms and forms of nature and the agricultural countryside, and was an astute chronicler of provincial England at the dawn of the industrial revolution. He possessed a passionate, inquisitive mind that sent him 'an itching after everything'.

He was born a twin on 13 July 1793, in Helpston, then a Northamptonshire village between Peterborough and Stamford on the edge of the Lincolnshire fens. His sister, seemingly the stronger twin, died after only a few weeks. His mother was illiterate and his farm labourer father could barely read – but did have a large repertoire of folk-songs which he liked to sing at local merrymakings.

As a boy of 10 Clare met Mary Joyce, the daughter of a prosperous farmer who didn't approve of the relationship. They parted in about 1816, and he never saw her again but her idealised presence remained with him to the end of his life. She became the muse of his creativity, associated in his memory with the happy landscape of his youth. She died unmarried in 1838 at the age of 41.

By the time he was 12, Clare's school-days were over. His father's health was failing and John had to earn money to support the family. He had various jobs working as a ploughboy,

John Clare in 1844, by the artist Thomas Grimshaw.

horseboy, reaper and thresher, pot boy at *The Blue Bell* inn, under-gardener and lime-burner.

At the age of 13 he read Thomson's *Seasons.* He was inspired to begin writing his own verses, but hid his first attempts from his parents. He persisted and soon began to think of publication. In 1819 his work was introduced to John Taylor, the publisher of Keats, and on 16 January 1820 Clare's first volume, *Poems Descriptive of Rural Life and Scenery,* was published, soon going into its fourth edition.

The Blue Bell *inn where Clare worked as a pot boy.*

Clare was a success – but only briefly. He visited London, met many famous writers, including Lamb and Hazlitt, and was acclaimed by the literary establishment. He found favour with the aristocracy and attracted a modest amount of patronage. Soon after, he married Martha Turner whom he knew as 'Patty'. She was never able to share his literary interests, but her love was to sustain him through the difficult years ahead. She was to bear him nine children.

As Clare was finding his literary voice, taste was turning from poetry to a more modern form of literature – the novel – and now the fickle public chose to ignore him. His second book, *The Village Minstrel,* appeared in 1821. His most ambitious poem, *The Shepherd's Calendar,* was finally published in 1827, but only after many frustrations and delays. Both sold badly and Clare quarrelled with his publisher over the editing of his work. He became demoralised. At the same time his womanising and drinking were getting out of hand. Often working away from home, his 'easy nature', as he put it, often led him into 'bad houses' and he developed a deep fear of catching venereal disease. No stranger to the bottle, he drank to ease the pressure

4

of straddling two worlds – the rustic and the literary – while being rejected by both.

In 1823 he showed the first signs of serious mental trouble and in May 1824 he visited London to consult Dr George Darling, who had earlier treated Keats. But, despite some temporary physical improvements, his health continued to fluctuate over

The cottage at Northborough.

the next few years and he fell more and more into debt. His friends and patrons arranged for him and his family to live as Lord Milton's tenants in a more comfortable cottage, which included two acres of land and an orchard, three miles away at Northborough. It was hoped that he would become self-supporting and that his health would improve. At first he was enthusiastic about the move but, as the day approached, he began to regret agreeing to it. He was then 39.

The family moved to Northborough in 1832 but Clare remained a stranger in his new home. During 1833-4 he tried without success to get *The Midsummer Cushion* published. In 1835 his last volume, *The Rural Muse,* was well received but did little to relieve his financial situation. Although he continued writing poetry his ambitions were effectively over and he began to suffer from memory loss and delusions. His health deteriorated and in 1837 Taylor, his publisher, arranged for him to enter a private asylum at Epping Forest near London.

For a while he responded well – his treatment was enlightened and he enjoyed considerable freedom. He wrote *Child Harold* and *Don Juan,* and said in a letter to his wife in November 1837, 'I am getting better'. Sadly, by 1841, his sense of identity was falling apart, and he suffered delusions that he was a prize fighter, Byron, Nelson, Burns, and Shakespeare, and that he had two wives, Patty and Mary.

Desperately unhappy, he fled the asylum in July 1841, and trudged home to Northborough on foot, covering the eighty miles in four days. His only sustenance on the journey was a half pint of beer on the second day, 'grass by the road side which seemed to taste something like bread' on the third day, and 'two half pints of ale and twopenn'oth of bread and cheese' on the fourth. The moving account of this journey, written after his return home, is a classic of autobiographical writing.

He stayed at home for five months, writing fitfully. His health was getting worse and he would fly into violent fits of temper. He was also given to brooding, mumbling to himself, and neglecting his responsibilities. Patty wanted to carry on caring for him but, days after his last Christmas at home, he reached the end of the road and was taken struggling to the Northampton General Lunatic Asylum. According to the certificate of application, he was suffering from 'years addicted to poetical prosings'. Clare wept, Patty wept, but the cottage at Northborough had seen the last of him.

'Midsummer cushions' of garden flowers laid at Clare's grave by local schoolchildren for the annual Clare Festival.
Midsummer cushions in John Clare's day were cushion-shaped boxes filled with wild flowers and were placed outside the cottages.

Clare remained in the Northampton Asylum until he died at the age of 71 on 20 May 1864. After his death his body was taken by train to Helpston where he was buried in the churchyard on 24 May.

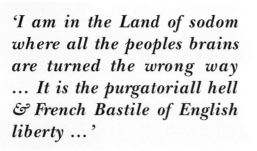

'I am in the Land of sodom where all the peoples brains are turned the wrong way ... It is the purgatoriall hell & French Bastile of English liberty ...'

6

St Andrew's Hospital, Northampton, was opened as the General Lunatic Asylum in 1838. Clare was taken to the asylum at the end of 1841 and ended his days there in 1864. Although admitted as a pauper patient, he was supported for the rest of his life by his most consistent patron, Lord Fitzwilliam. This support allowed Clare to enjoy some of the privileges of being a private patient – he had, for instance, a room of his own. Dr Prichard, the superintendent, classified him as harmless, and in the early years he was allowed to wander the surrounding countryside and the town almost at will, returning only for meals and bed. *The Northampton Mercury,* 30 April 1842, reported that Clare 'may be seen any fine day, walking, with a rapid step and an abstracted manner, about the grounds of the asylum, one hand in his pocket and the other in the bosom of his waistcoat, easily distinguishable by the most careless observer as no ordinary man'. Sometimes he would sit and gaze at the sky as in a trance. His physical health improved, though not his state of mind.

Clare continued to compose poetry and there was some good fortune, for posterity certainly, in the appointment in April 1845 of W F Knight as House Steward to the asylum. He took a keen interest in Clare, befriended him,

St Andrew's Hospital as it is today – virtually unchanged since Clare's time.

encouraged his creativity and began the task of transcribing into two large volumes over 800 poems, the bulk of the asylum poetry: 'Copied from the Manuscripts as presented to me by Clare – and favoured with others by some Ladies and Gentlemen, that Clare had presented them to'. When Knight left for Birmingham in 1850, the work was continued by other, unknown, copyists.

As the years went by Clare's movements had to be more and more restricted. He went through bad periods when he became abusive and obscene, or violent, when he would have been a danger outside. On at least one occasion he was kept in through no fault of his own. Knight wrote in a letter dated 3 March 1846: 'You will be sorry to hear that poor John Clare is not allowed to go out of the walls of this place – for on Saturday last he went into town and someone made him intoxicated – for this he is incarcerated'.

Dr Prichard, Superintendent at St Andrew's at the time of Clare's admission.

No matter how sympathetic and accommodating Dr Prichard and his successors Dr P R Nesbitt (1845-60) and Dr E Wing (1860-65) could be, Clare's tortured mind could only see himself as a helpless captive, as we can read in a letter to his wife, 19 July 1848: 'I am in the Land of sodom where all the peoples brains are turned the wrong way ... I write this in a green meadow by the side of the river agen Stokes Mill & I see three of your daughters & a Son now and then   the confusion & roar of Mill dams & locks is sounding very pleasant while I write it & its a very beautiful Evening   the meadows are greener than usual after the shower & the Rivers are brimful   I think it is about two years since I was first sent up in this hell & not allowed to go out of the

8

The chapel at St Andrew's which Clare may have visited during his final days.

Clare was often limited to the grounds of St Andrew's but still found himself close to nature.

gates   there never was a more disgraceful deception than this place. It is the purgatoriall hell & French Bastile of English liberty …'

Almost to the very end of his days, Clare never lost his dignity and distinguished looks. The last months of his slow physical and mental decline are charted in Dr Wing's case-book: 'February 1st 1863: Became very giddy and appeared to lose the use of his legs just before dinner time today, so he was put to bed. His delusions about his personal identity are as strong as ever, sometimes fancying himself Lord Byron, at others a Sea Captain, etc. His language is at times very bad.'

He wrote his last poem about six months before his death and the casebook for 20 May reads: 'This morning on being visited he was found to be completely comatose and never rallied but died quietly late in the afternoon.'

There is no doubt that Clare was mentally ill, and there are many descriptions of his state of mind at different periods of his life, written by himself or by people who knew him, including in his later years visitors to the asylum and his physicians. These descriptions have been interpreted in different ways and there is no agreed diagnosis. Some say that he had a 'manic depressive' disorder, in which moods swing between excessively active high spirits and very inactive low spirits; others say he was 'schizo-phrenic', pointing to his delusions and his withdrawn moods; he may have had cerebral syphilis, which could account for what became crippling inertia in his last years.

A surviving twin, he was born bereaved; he was frail and anxious and had frequent 'blackouts'; he may have suffered from malaria. His education set him apart socially; his imagination was peopled by spirits of an almost medieval mythology which could frighten him even in sophisticated London, where he dreaded being pursued by 'terribles ... goblins with saucer eyes'. He was always unlucky – in love, and in his chosen vocation – and because of this he felt persecuted. He was very much a hypochondriac. He was given to excessive drinking, and to womanising – he could have contracted venereal disease; he probably suffered from malnutrition. His illness seemed to change its nature in mid-life from one which was psychological – a developing personality, which was inherently sensitive responding to an overload of stresses – to one which was more obviously physical. The cause of his death was cerebrovascular disease.

At St Andrew's Clare often sat for portraits, including this, the only photograph of him (Mr Law 1862).

Whatever the label we give to his illness, if we are looking for causes there were surely many contributory factors in a life driven by all sorts of tensions, stresses and contradictions, emotional, economic, vocational, physical, none resolvable except in the act of writing poem after poem. ❧

> *Inclosure came and*
> *trampled on the grave*
> *Of labours rights and*
> *left the poor a slave*
>
> from 'The Mores'

Clare's is one of the few voices among the rural poor to come to us directly across two centuries telling, in verse and prose, of the social and economic changes as they affected the agricultural labourer and the structure of rural society.

Clare's verse grew out of popular culture, the oral tradition of songs and tales, chapbooks and ballads and broadsides. The rhythms of folksong and the language of dialect abound in his original poetry, and among his poems are his own versions of many traditional ballads. He became the first serious collector of English folk material. In true folk tradition, Clare has left a vivid record of village customs and pastimes, of ballad singers and morris dancers, a whole cast of village characters.

When Clare was growing up in Helpston the farming community was a traditional one. It was based upon the medieval 'open field' system of agriculture: three large fields divided into acre strips, a varying number of which were owned by each family and scattered throughout the fields. There were no dividing fences and there was a criss-cross of access paths. An area of 'common land' was used by all for grazing animals and collecting fuel and building materials. Farming was a communal affair – labour and tools were shared – and it imparted a social unity: people worked together, and together observed time-honoured customs.

But in England at large a new age was burgeoning which brought radical change to this traditional lifestyle. Wealthy landowners, including successful new industrialists who had bought land, wanted to invest in new, more productive

Morris dancers at Helpston.

farming methods to meet the demands of a growing and urban-ising population. New methods were incompatible with the open field system: the answer was enclosure. This involved combining land strips into large fields with *one* owner and *separated* by fences. It could be achieved by private agreement, as it had been for centuries in some parts, or by Act of Parliament. The latter, though expensive, was a quick method and was freely used by the wealthy who stood to make big gains. Unfortunately, enclosures were carried out in a spirit of commercial-ism and with scant regard for the wishes of farm labourers who, because they were poor, had no redress. By 1815 farmlands were owned by a wealthy minority, while poorer folk became labourers or, at best, tenant farmers. The cottagers who had never owned a strip lost the use of common land.

A map of Helpston showing the enclo-sure boundaries.

The country labourer was now dependent upon a weekly wage for subsistence – and wages were low. The cost of bread, however, was high, inflation in grain prices being fuelled by the Napoleonic Wars (1793–1815). Helpston was enclosed in 1809 and in 1810 the average wage was about five shillings (25p) a week; a four-pound loaf of bread cost one shilling (5p). The ranks of those in need of Poor Law relief were swelled. The 'Speenhamland System' of poor relief, origi-nating in Berkshire, had become widespread. It was an income supplement linked to the price of bread and the size of a man's family, and it was paid from parish rates.

Clare bore agonised witness to the overthrow of the social order of the past, and with it the loss of the old honesty and integrity as wealth became the yardstick of success. Village sports and customs were also disappearing as a result of enclosure. There arose a new breed of upstart farmer who scorned the tradition and no longer sat down with his men at the supper table at harvest time. No wonder Clare saw everyone involved in the destruction of his native fields as enemies. The parish officers who administered the Poor Law showed about as much humanity and mercy as the new farmers. Under this system farmers had little incentive to pay a realistic wage and the genuine hardworking labourer had to suffer the indignity of a parish handout. In Clare's words, 'Work for the little I choose to allow you and go to the parish for the rest – or starve.'

THE "MILK" OF POOR-LAW "KINDNESS."

The Poor Law satirised by Punch.

These things John Clare experienced and recorded, and in this he was doubly alienated: from sophisticated new-age society because he was a peasant and from peasant society because he was a most literate man. Nothing more clearly illustrates the growing difference between the cultures of country and town than a comparison of the poet and his publisher. Taylor was the polished, shrewd intellectual, a representative of the modern spirit of progress. Clare was the earth-born child, lover of simple things, a survivor of an England that was dying. His lyrical poems, in which people live in harmony with each other and with nature, are the swansongs of that mythical England. ❦

I took a walk today to botanize ...

letter from Clare 25 March 1825

The greatest happiness of Clare's life was centred in his intimate knowledge of the countryside around Helpston. To the north and east of the village was fenland, and to the south and west were woods and heathland. He once said that he found his poems in the fields and simply wrote them down.

Clare read widely in natural history, but his detailed knowledge as a naturalist derived primarily from patient fieldwork, closely watching the activities and habitats of animals and plants and recording his observations in notebooks. It is this precise observation that both enabled Clare to identify with the myriad forms of nature and to understand the relationships between living things. It also makes him one of the foremost nature poets in the English language. Other poets looked at landscape as if from outside, but Clare was part of it and vividly illuminates it in poetry using local words and expressions. The same gentleness and love for the living world that Clare exhibits in his poetry made physical violence and cruelty abhorrent to him. He refused to join his fellow villagers in poaching and badger-baiting; nor did he collect specimens to put them, dead, into glass cases, condemning 'the fashionable folly to gibbet butterflyes & strangle beetles'.

On 4 June 1825 Clare's journal records his meeting with some workmen who were 'laying out the plan for an "Iron railway" from Manchester to London ... I little thought that fresh intrusions woud interupt & spoil my solitudes after the Inclosure they will despoil a boggy

'I never pass a venerable tree, pining away into nothingness and dust ...'

14

Wild orchids can still be found at Royce Wood today, despite the railway.

place that is famous for Orchises at Royce Wood end.' The enclosure of land, the introduction of mechanisation in farming and the 'fresh intrusions' of an industrialising society, swept away a landscape and a whole way of life that had endured for centuries. Clare saw the uprooting of trees and the felling of whole woods, the diverting of streams from their courses, commons fenced off and 'No Trespassing' notices posted, the destruction of the village green, heaths and moors going under the plough, the disappearance of footpaths and wildlife habitats, and the drainage of the fens. In verse and prose he denounced the newly systematised and efficient agriculture not only for its effect on poor agricultural labourers, dispossessed of their rights, but also for its assault on the land itself – each field, fen and tree – and its creatures, evicted from their homes and denied the freedom to roam.

If you go to Helpston today you will not find the countryside that Clare so loved. Much of the surrounding fenland, then extending clear down to the Lincolnshire coast, has been reclaimed for development or agriculture and in Northamptonshire nearly all the meadows and heathland have now disappeared. The wildlife of the area, as elsewhere, represents but a fraction of what once existed. In England as a whole, the effects of modern society have, each year, resulted in a net loss of hedgerows, an important wildlife habitat.

A modern agricultural landscape without hedgerows.

Changes in agricultural practices, particularly since 1945, and continuing pressures from development have drastically changed the nature of our countryside. Clare saw the birth of a mechanised agricultural system that tipped the ecological balance, culminating in today's 'industrial' farming with its use of chemicals and intensive methods of production. At the same time, the Industrial Revolution resulted in an escalation of urban development creating the need for more roads, railways and industry. As a consequence of this modernisation, quarrying, river pollution from both sewage and industrial waste and air pollution have now become constant threats to nature. Scientists report on the mounting evidence of the effects of all this 'progress': if we do not redress the balance, we may reap a bitter harvest. Ultimately the fate of our environment rests on the attitudes and actions of people. Wise management – putting conservation at the heart of land-use policies – and increased awareness can help. Conservation bodies and caring landowners have done much to redress the balance and national nature reserves like Barnack 'Hills and Holes' show what can be done to preserve the countryside.

Barnack 'Hills and Holes', which Clare knew well, is now a national nature reserve.

John Clare rejoiced in everything that the modern obsession with progress and profit would destroy. He was a pantheist, in the sense that he regarded nature as God's creation, and everything in it as sacred. Curiously, he was even labelled a 'Green Man' in his own lifetime by some of his literary acquaintances. Eric Robinson writes: 'Clare was a brilliant observer of the natural scene ... a major figure both in poetry and in natural-history writing – a prophet who can guide us into the next century.' ❦

I would not that
* my being all should die*
& pass away
* with every common lot*

from 'Memory'

Memorial plaque to John Clare in Poet's Corner, Westminster Abbey.

For all the lionising, Clare was regarded in his own day as a minor figure. What appealed was not so much the poetry, but the phenomenon of Clare the Northamptonshire Peasant Poet or, a little later, the Mad Poet. The canon of early 19th-century romantic poetry was soon fixed as Wordsworth and Coleridge, Keats, Byron and Shelley. Only during the last fifty years or so has it been whispered abroad that a sixth name should be added to the list, that of John Clare.

That he ever became a poet is nothing short of a miracle. The odds were stacked against him. That he persisted and became one of England's most prolific poets is even more miraculous. After all, his life was an unmitigated disaster.

Yet Clare was primarily a happy poet. He loved his childhood and nature in all its manifestations, he loved human life, especially when part of the natural scene, and he loved poetry, old ballads, village customs and rural occupations. Much of his poetry – that inspired by emotional recall of characters and scenes from his childhood – is sheer celebration. His life, though, was fraught with

from 'Enclosure'

Like mighty giants of their limbs bereft,
The skybound wastes in mangled garbs are left,
Fence meeting fence in owner's little bounds
Of field and meadow, large as garden-grounds,
In little parcels little minds to please,
With men and flocks imprisoned, ill at ease.
For with the poor scared freedom bade farewell,
And fortune-hunters totter where they fell;
They dreamed of riches in the rebel scheme
And find too truly that they did but dream.

'I AM'

1

I am — yet what I am, none cares or knows;
    My friends forsake me like a memory lost: —
I am the self-consumer of my woes; —
    They rise and vanish in oblivion's host,
Like shadows in love's frenzied stifled throes: —
And yet I am, and live — like vapours tost

2

Into the nothingness of scorn and noise, —
    Into the living sea of waking dreams,
Where there is neither sense of life or joys,
    But the vast shipwreck of my lifes esteems;
Even the dearest, that I love the best
Are strange — nay, rather stranger than the rest.

3

I long for scenes, where man hath never trod
    A place where woman never smiled or wept
There to abide with my Creator, God;
    And to sleep as I in childhood, sweetly slept,
Untroubling, and untroubled where I lie,
The grass below — above the vaulted sky.

many problems, and inevitably there entered into his poetry a more sombre tone, brought about by loss and change, destruction and isolation, and the less benign aspects of his own experience.

Clare had a responsive and intuitive nature and he never submitted to using artificial poetic language to suit the affected taste of the drawing room as his patrons might have liked but continued to write in his own way – straight from the heart. He was a poet of great truth and power, and his genius had tremendous range: poems of nature observation – trees and birds especially, love songs, ballads, satire, sonnets, superb lyrical and narrative poems, intense metaphysical poems.

In Clare's poetry (and prose), punctuation is usually absent and spelling and syntax do not always follow standard practice.

18

Hares at Play

The birds are gone to bed the cows are still
And sheep lie panting on each old mole hill
And underneath the willows grey-green bough
Like toil a resting—lies the fallow plough
The timid hares throw daylight fears away
On the lanes road to dust and dance and play
Then dabble in the grain by nought deterred
To lick the dewfall from the barleys beard
Then out they sturt again and round the hill
Like happy thoughts—dance—squat—and loiter still
Till milking maidens in the early morn
Gingle their yokes and sturt them in the corn
Through well known beaten paths each nimbling hare
Sturts quick as fear—and seeks its hidden lair

The Setting Sun

This scene how beautious to the musing mind
That now swift slides from an enchanting view
The Sun sweet setting yon far hills behind
In other worlds his Visits to renew
What spangling glories all around him shine
What nameless colours cloudles[s] and serene
(A heavnly prospect brightest in decline)
Attend his exit from this lovely scene—
—So sets the christians sun in glories clear
So shines his soul at his departure here
No clouding doubts nor misty fears arise
To dim hopes golden rays of being forgiven
His sun sweet setting in the clearest skyes
In safe assurance wings the soul to heaven—

This is because editors today prefer to present Clare as far as possible as he wrote and do not feel justified in 'correcting' him. This was not always the case. Taylor and Hessey, his first publishers, did not hesitate to tidy him up to suit polite literary taste of the period. Provincialisms, dialect words, vulgarisms were omitted or replaced by more acceptable language. Any sentiments thought politically or morally offensive were censored. Whole sections of *The Shepherd's Calendar* were left out or rewritten. Yet many of Clare's grammatical omissions were deliberate – 'do I write intelligable   I am genneraly understood tho I do not use that awkward squad of pointings called commas colons semicolons etc' – and adding it later, instead of aiding our understanding, often just impedes the flow of the verse.

Today we can read what Clare wrote as he wrote it. There is no need to condescend to him as his patrons and mentors did. His native vigour and healthy robustness, his directness of expression, his evocativeness, his accuracy, his distinctive voice, his truth and integrity, all come through more powerfully than ever. ❧

To Mary

1

I sleep with thee, and wake with thee,
And yet thou art not there:—
I fill my arms, with thoughts of thee,
And press the common air.—
Thy eyes are gazing upon mine,
When thou art out of sight;
My lips are always touching thine,
At morning, noon, and night.

2

I think, and speak of other things,
To keep my mind at rest:
But still to thee, my memory clings,
Like love in womans breast;—
I hide it from the worlds-wide eye;
And think, and speak contrary;
But soft, the wind comes from the sky,
And wispers tales of Mary.—

3

The night wind wispers in my ear,
The moon shines in my face;
A burden still of chilling fear,
I find in every place.—
The breeze is wispering in the bush;
And the dew-fall from the tree,
All; sighing on, and will not hush,
Some pleasant tales of thee.—

The North Fen Road near Glinton, where Clare used to meet Mary Joyce.

19

20

John Clare Monument and St Botolph's Church, Helpston.

Lolham Bridges, where Patty met Clare after his escape from the asylum at Epping Forest.

On the trail of John Clare a visit to the beautiful village of Helpston, some seven miles north-west of Peterborough, is essential. Clare was born here, and his life's experience was centred within a small radius of it. His intimate perception of the life of this locality, both natural and social, influenced all his writing. At Helpston can be seen Clare's cottage (which is privately owned – the garden *only* is open during the Clare Festival), *The Blue Bell* inn and *The Exeter Arms,* which is where his body rested overnight before burial. His grave is on the south-east side of St Botolph's churchyard, and opposite the Buttercross is the Clare Memorial with its inscription about the posthumous fame of the poet.

Within a four-mile radius of Helpston lies a cluster of villages which Clare knew well: east to Glinton, where Clare went to school; north to Maxey and Northborough, where the cottage in which Clare's family lived from 1832 can still be seen. As a working lad, Clare often went to Maxey, taking corn from Helpston to be ground at the flour mill there. Today, Maxey Mill is restored to full working order and can sometimes be visited. Barnack and Ashton lie to the west and a little further Stamford, which has many Clare associations. Clare loved the walk to Barnack, especially to the 'Hills and Holes' on its south-west edge – a large area of mounds and hollows formed out of long-disused stone quarries. It is now a nature reserve, an unspoilt area good for walking. Near Stamford is Burghley where Clare worked as a gardener; and beyond, in his days as a lime-burner, Clare became familiar with Casterton, Ryhall, Tickencote and Pickworth, where the lime kiln has recently been restored and is open to the public. At Tickencote he frequented *The Flower Pot* inn (now a house) and at Oundle, after briefly joining the militia in 1812, he was billeted at *The Rose and Crown* in the town centre.

Clare's cottage at Helpston.

The visitor to Northampton will wish to see the Clare Collection held at the Central Library, Abington Street (see p.22), and the museum in Guildhall Road, which has a pair of black laced shoes, and hair-brush and comb, used by Clare at the asylum. Clare was a familiar figure around Northampton – he regularly walked to town from St Andrew's (today a private hospital on the Billing Road) and some of the poems he wrote during this period, now in the Clare collection, are addressed to girls he met in his strolls. He would sit for hours in the portico of All Saints' Church at the heart of town watching the world pass by, or talking to local people and occasionally writing verses for them in exchange for some chewing tobacco. It is fitting that Tom Bates's bust of the poet was installed inside All Saints' in 1993. George Maine's portrait of Clare, 1848, shows him, pen and book in hand, sitting there in the shadows of the portico, surely Northampton's most poignant memory of the 'countryside poet'. ❦

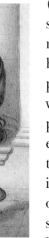

The portrait by George Maine.

Some months after Clare's funeral John Taylor, the Northampton bookseller and no relation to Clare's publisher, bought the poet's books and papers from his widow at Northborough. He had to hire two donkeys and carts to transport all the material to the station.

Taylor's purchase forms the heart of the Collection housed in the Local Studies Collection at the Northamptonshire Central Library, Abington Street, Northampton. It contains manuscript sources, hundreds of his letters and his library, preserved almost intact and consisting of some 440 volumes.

The Collection is especially strong in material from the asylum period including the Knight transcripts. Here also are Clare's arithmetic school book (1803), his journal for 1824-5 and notebooks kept at High Beech Asylum, Epping Forest and on his long walk home to Northborough. There are likenesses of Clare in painted portraits (Thomas Grimshaw, 1844; George Maine 1848), in photograph (Mr Law, 1862), and in sculpture (Henry Behnes, 1828).

The bust by Henry Behnes.

The Collection continues to grow with the addition of new works about Clare and reviews and articles from periodicals as they appear. The library welcomes donations or information on material which may have been overlooked.

The Clare Collection can be visited during normal library opening hours but it is advisable to write or telephone (0604 26774) first so that any special arrangements can be made. Microfilm copies of the manuscripts are available for consultation, and microfilm readers can be booked in advance. Catalogues of the John Clare Collection are available from the library. ❦

PUBLISHED EDITIONS OF HIS WORKS

Grainger, M. The Natural History Prose Writings of John Clare
(Oxford University Press, 1983)

Robinson, E. John Clare's Autobiographical Writings
(Oxford University Press, 1983)

Robinson, E. and Powell, D. The Early Poems of John Clare,
1804-22, 2 vols.
(Oxford University Press, 1989)

Robinson, E. and Powell, D. The Later Poems of John Clare,
1837-64, 2 vols.
(Oxford University Press, 1984)

Robinson, E. and Powell, D. The Oxford Authors John Clare
(Oxford University Press, 1984)

Robinson, E., Powell, D. and Dowson, P. Cottage Tales
(Mid Northumberland Arts Group and Carcanet Press, 1993)

Robinson, E., Powell, D. and Summerfield G. The Shepherd's
Calendar
(Oxford University Press, 1993)

Storey, M. The Letters of John Clare
(Oxford University Press, 1985)

Summerfield, G. John Clare, Selected Poetry
(Penguin, 1990)

Thornton, R.K.R. and Tibble, A. John Clare, The Midsummer
Cushion
(Mid Northumberland Arts Group and Carcanet Press, 1990)

Thornton, R.K.R. The Rural Muse, poems by John Clare
(Mid Northumberland Arts Group and Carcanet Press, 1983)

23

BIOGRAPHIES AND CRITICAL WORKS

Barrell, J. The Idea of Landscape and the Sense of Place, 1730–1840: an approach to the poetry of John Clare
(Cambridge University Press, 1972)

Brownlow, T. John Clare and the Picturesque Landscape
(Oxford University Press, 1983)

Chilcott, T. 'A Real World & Doubting Mind', a critical study of the poetry of John Clare
(Hull University Press, 1985)

Clare, Johanne. John Clare and the Bounds of Circumstance
(McGill – Queens University Press, 1987)

Deacon, G. John Clare and the Folk Tradition
(Sinclair Browne, 1983)

The John Clare Society Journal 1982 and annually

Martin, F.W. The Life of John Clare, 2nd ed., with an introduction and notes by E. Robinson and G. Summerfield
(Frank Cass, 1964)

Storey, E. A Right to Song: the life of John Clare
(Methuen, 1982)

Storey, M. The Poetry of John Clare: a critical introduction
(Macmillan, 1974)

Tibble, J.W. and A. John Clare: his life and poetry
(Heinemann, 1956)